LONDON & SYDNEY

London et Sydney Explorent Le Monde: Texas

Ce Livre Est À

Copyright © 2018 by Kellen Coleman

All rights reserved. This book or any portion thereof may not be reproduced or used in any manner whatsoever without the express written permission of the publisher except for the use of brief quotations in a book review.

ISBN 978-0998892979

Visit us at LondonandSydney.com

FOMENKYPUBLISHING.COM

Layout by Brandon Richardson

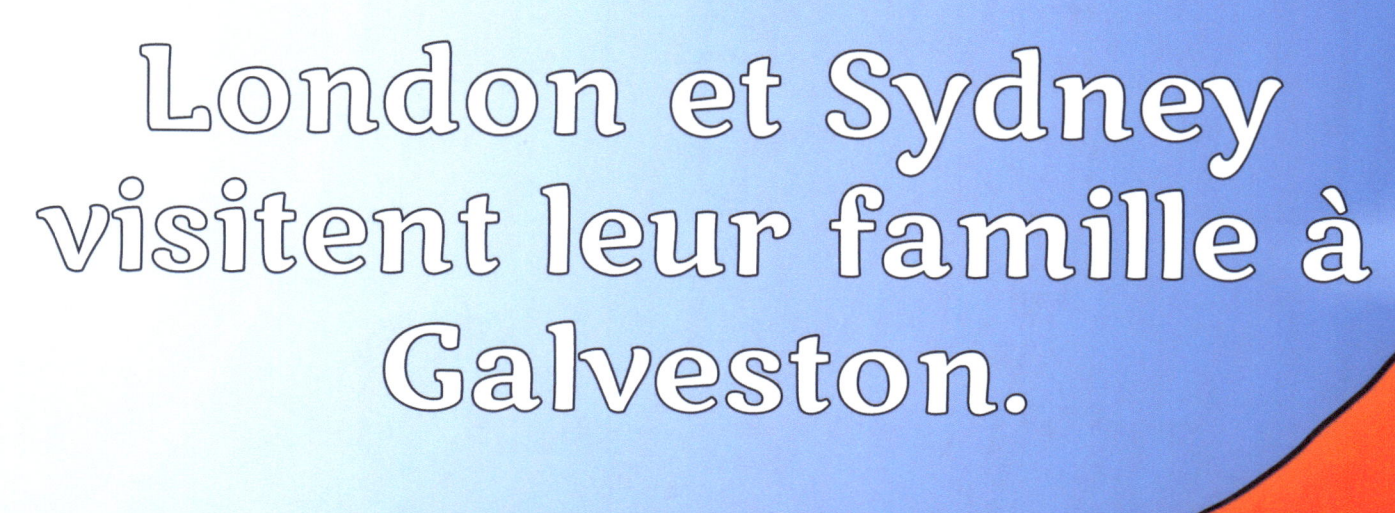

London et Sydney visitent leur famille à Galveston.

À El Paso, London et Sydney comptent les étoiles près de la Fontaine,

regardent une grande étoile sur la montagne Franklin.

Disent, allons au Mexique!